"PYTHON RELEASED: BECOMING THE BEST AT PROGRAMMING"

2

Contents

Forward

Python is a flexible and famous programming language that has acquired boundless utilize both globally and locally, going with it a fantastic decision for people in different fields, including essayists and distributers such as yourself. In this human-composed text, we will give a prologue to Python, examine the justifications for why learning Python can be valuable, and guide you through setting up your Python climate.

What is Python?

Python is an undeniable level, deciphered programming language known for its meaningfulness and straightforwardness. It was made by Guido van Rossum and first delivered in 1991. Python is known for its spotless and straightforward sentence structure, which looks like the English language. This pursues it an extraordinary decision for fledglings and experienced developers the same.

Python is an open-source language, and that implies it is uninhibitedly accessible for anybody to utilize and circulate. It has a huge and dynamic local area of designers who constantly add to its development, bringing about a broad library of modules and bundles for different purposes.

Why Learn Python?

As an essayist and distributer, there are a few convincing justifications for why learning Python can be helpful:

Mechanizing Dull Undertakings: Python permits you to computerize tedious and dreary errands, like information passage, record the board, and text handling. This can save your time for additional innovative undertakings.

Information Investigation and Representation: Python has strong libraries like Pandas, NumPy, and Matplotlib that empower you to break down information and make representations, which can be significant for exploration and content creation.

Web Improvement: Python can be utilized for web advancement with systems like Django and Cup, assisting you with making sites and online stages to advance your work.

Normal Language Handling (NLP): Python's NLP libraries like NLTK and spaCy are astounding devices for message examination, opinion investigation, and language handling, which can be significant for scholars and distributers.

Cross-Stage Similarity: Python is accessible on different stages, guaranteeing that your work is open to a wide crowd.

Setting up Python Climate

To get everything rolling with Python, you'll have to set up your Python climate. Here are the fundamental stages:

Learning Assets: Investigate online instructional exercises, books, and courses to learn Python. Consider stages like Codecademy, Coursera, or edX, which offer exhaustive Python courses.

Practice: Begin composing Python code to rehearse and support your insight. Python's intuitive nature makes it an extraordinary language for learning through trial and error.

All in all, Python is a flexible programming language that can enormously help essayists and distributers, offering mechanization capacities, information examination instruments, web improvement choices, and the sky is the limit from there. Setting up your Python climate is the most important move toward utilizing Python's ability to improve your work and efficiency. Go ahead and request more unambiguous subtleties or help with any part of Python you might want to investigate further.

Getting everything moving with Python:

Python is an adaptable and comprehensively used programming language. Its perfect and easy to-examine etymological design goes with it an incredible choice for juveniles. To start, you'll must have Python presented on your PC. You can download it from the power Python webpage (python.org).

You're Most important Python Program:

Could we start by making your outright first Python program. Open a word processor (like Journal) and make one more record with a ".py" extension. For instance, you can name it "my_first_program.py."

In this record, you can start with an essential "Hello there, World!"

python

Copy code

```python
print("Hello, World!")
```

Save the archive and open your terminal or request brief. Investigate to the envelope where you saved your Python report and run it using the going with request:

Copy code

```
python my_first_program.py
```

You'll see the outcome "Hey, World!" on your screen. Congratulations! You've as of late executed your most significant Python program.

Elements and Data Types:

Python grants you to work with various data types, for instance, numbers, floating point numbers, strings, and anything is possible from that point. You can similarly portray variables to store data.

Here is an occurrence of describing elements and showing their characteristics:

python
Copy code
```python
# Elements and data types
age = 30 # an entire number
level = 1.75 # a float
name = "John" # a string

# Printing factors
print("Name:", name)
print("Age:", age)
```

```python
print("Height:", level)
```

This code portrays factors for age, level, and name and prints their characteristics.

Major Data and Result:

Python moreover allows relationship with the client through data and result. You can use the information() capacity to get client data and print() to show information.

Here is a model:

python
Copy code

These are just the real basics of Python programming. As you dive further into Python, you can explore additional puzzling subjects and libraries for various applications, including data assessment, web progression, and that is just a glimpse of something larger. An adaptable gadget can overhaul your piece and dispersing limits by means of motorizing tasks and analyzing data, truth is told.

Restrictive Explanations (if, elif, else)

Contingent proclamations are utilized to go with choices in your code. They permit you to execute various blocks of code in view of whether certain circumstances are met. Here is an outline:

if proclamation: It really takes a look at a condition and executes a block of code in the event that the condition is valid. For instance:

```python
Duplicate code
if condition:
    # Code to execute assuming that
the condition is valid
```

elif proclamation: Means "else if." It's utilized to actually look at extra circumstances if the underlying 'if' condition is bogus. For instance:

python
Duplicate code

```python
in the event that condition1:
    # Code to execute assuming that condition1 is valid
elif condition2:
    # Code to execute on the off chance that condition2 is valid
```

else articulation: This is utilized with an 'if' proclamation to execute code assuming the underlying condition is bogus. For instance:

python
Duplicate code

```python
in the event that condition:
    # Code to execute assuming the condition is valid
else:
```

```
    # Code to execute on the off chance that the condition is misleading
```

3.2 Circles (for and keeping in mind that)

Circles are utilized to rehash a block of code on numerous occasions. There are two essential sorts of circles in Python:

for circle: It's pre-owned when you need to emphasize over a grouping (like a rundown or a scope of numbers) and play out a similar activity for everything in the succession. For instance:

Python
Duplicate code
```
for thing in succession:
    # Code to execute for everything in the grouping
```

while circle: This circle keeps executing up to a specific condition is valid. It's not unexpected utilized when you don't have the foggiest idea how frequently you really want to rehash a block of code. For instance:

```python
Duplicate code
while condition:
    # Code to execute while the condition is valid
```

Control Stream Activities

To dominate these ideas, you can rehearse with works out. Here are a few models:

Compose a Python program that checks assuming a given number is even or odd utilizing restrictive proclamations.

Make a circle that prints the numbers from 1 to 10 utilizing a for circle.

Foster a program that requests that the client enter their age utilizing some time circle. Continue to ask until they enter a legitimate age (e.g., somewhere in the range of 1 and 100).

These activities will assist you with turning out to be more capable in control stream designs and upgrade your programming abilities.

Go ahead and request more subtleties or models connected with these ideas or particular activities you might want to investigate further.

Python offers a few underlying information structures, each filling a particular need:

•	Lists: Records are requested assortments of things, and they can store different information types. They are signified by square sections, for example, [1, 2, 3]. Records are alterable, and that implies you can add, eliminate, or change components.

•	Tuples: Tuples are like records, yet they are permanent, meaning their components can't be changed after creation. They are characterized utilizing enclosures, e.g., (1, 2, 3).

•	Dictionaries: Word references utilize key-esteem matches to store information. They are encased in wavy supports and have the configuration {'key': ' value'}. Word references are especially valuable for quick queries.

• Sets: Sets are unordered assortments of one of kind components. They are characterized with wavy supports or the set() constructor. For instance, {1, 2, 3}.

• Strings: Strings are arrangements of characters. They are likewise an information structure in Python, and you can control them very much like different information structures.

• Arrays: Python has a cluster module that permits you to make and control exhibits. Clusters are more memory-productive than records while managing enormous datasets of a solitary information type.

• Stacks and Lines: These are dynamic information types that can be carried out utilizing records. Stacks follow the Rearward In-First-Out (LIFO) guideline, while lines follow the Earliest in, earliest out (FIFO) rule.

• Connected Records: Connected records are a basic information structure in software engineering. They comprise of hubs associated with one another, and they can be utilized to execute different information structures like stacks, lines, and the sky is the limit from there.

•	Trees and Diagrams: Trees and charts are progressive information structures. Trees have a solitary root hub with kid hubs, while diagrams comprise of hubs associated by edges. They are utilized in many applications, including sorting out various leveled information and organization displaying.

•	Custom Information Designs: Notwithstanding implicit information structures, Python permits you to make custom information structures custom fitted to your particular necessities. This can be accomplished through classes and articles.

• While expounding on information structures, it's fundamental to make sense of their qualities, use cases, and give code guides to represent how they work. You can likewise investigate calculations and tasks related with every information structure. This natty gritty methodology will make your substance instructive and drawing in for your peruses.

• Make sure to stay away from copyright infringement by referring to sources assuming you're utilizing data from different journalists, and give unique experiences and clarifications to make your substance exceptional and important.

Capabilities in Python:

Capabilities are crucial structure blocks in Python. Consider them reusable code pieces that play out a particular undertaking. They are characterized utilizing the def catchphrase, trailed by the capability name and enclosures. Here is a fundamental model:

```python
Duplicate code
def greet(name):
    print("Hello, " + name)

greet("Alice")
```

In this model, we characterize a capability welcome that takes one contention, name, and prints a hello. At the point when we call greet("Alice"), it prints "Hi, Alice."

Capabilities can return values too. For instance:

```python
Duplicate code
def add(a, b):
    return a + b

result = add(3, 4)
print(result) # This will print 7
```

Capabilities are pivotal for code association, reusability, and keeping a clean codebase.

Modules in Python:

Modules in Python are records containing Python code. They can characterize capabilities, classes, and factors. Python's standard library is an assortment of modules that give a large number of functionalities. You can likewise make your own modules.

For example, on the off chance that you have a document named my_module.py with the accompanying substance:

```python
Duplicate code
def say_hello(name):
    return "Hi, " + name

my_variable = 42
```

You can involve this module in another Python script:

```python
Duplicate code
import my_module

result = my_module.say_hello("Bob")
print(result) # This will print "Hi, Sway"

print(my_module.my_variable)  # This will print 42
```

Modules assist you with coordinating code into isolated records, making it more straightforward to oversee enormous activities and offer code with others.

Utilizing Capabilities from Modules:

You can likewise characterize capabilities in modules and use them in your code. For instance, on the off chance that you have a module math_operations.py:

python
Duplicate code

```python
def multiply(a, b):
  return a * b
```

You can involve this capability in another content:

python
Duplicate code

```python
import math_operations

result = math_operations.multiply(5, 6)
print(result) # This will print 30
```

This is a fundamental outline of capabilities and modules in Python. They are fundamental for making coordinated, reusable, and proficient code. As an essayist and distributer, you could find it valuable to make sense of these ideas obviously while expounding on Python programming for your crowd.

Classes and Articles:

In OOP, a class resembles a diagram or a layout for making objects. An item, then again, is a case of a class. Consider a class a recipe and an item as the genuine dish arranged utilizing that recipe.

We should dive further into the critical components of OOP in Python:

Encapsulation: This idea includes packaging the information (credits) and the strategies (works) that work on the information into a solitary unit called a class. This helps hold related usefulness together, advancing spotless and coordinated code.

Inheritance: Legacy permits one class to acquire characteristics and techniques from another class. This advances code reuse and the production of additional particular classes. For example, you can have a nonexclusive "Vehicle" class and afterward make explicit classes like "Vehicle" and "Bicycle" that acquire qualities from the "Vehicle" class.

Polymorphism: This is about the capacity of various classes to be treated as cases of a typical superclass. It empowers you to compose more conventional code that can work with different sorts of articles.

Abstraction: Deliberation improves on complex reality by displaying classes in light of their fundamental elements, while concealing the superfluous subtleties. It resembles utilizing a controller without knowing how the internal hardware functions. You don't have to know the complex subtleties to really utilize it.

We should show these ideas with a straightforward Python code model:

```python
Duplicate code
class Creature:
    def __init__(self, name):
        self.name = name

    def speak(self):
        pass

class Dog(Animal):
    def speak(self):
        return f"{self.name} says Woof!"

class Cat(Animal):
    def speak(self):
        return f"{self.name} says Whimper!"

# Making objects
canine = Dog("Buddy")
feline = Cat("Whiskers")
```

Utilizing polymorphism to call the talk strategy

for creature in [dog, cat]:
   print(animal.speak())
In this model, we have a base class Creature with a talk strategy, and two subclasses, Canine and Feline, each giving their own execution of talk. This exhibits legacy and polymorphism.

As an essayist and distributer, you can make sense of these ideas in a manner that is open to your peruses, giving genuine models and commonsense applications. Understanding OOP is critical for any software engineer, and your capacity to convey these ideas obviously will be an important resource in your composition and distributing tries.

Record Taking care of in Python

Python offers a few underlying capabilities and strategies for record dealing with. These abilities permit you to peruse from and write to documents, which is particularly valuable for handling and overseeing text or information that you work with in your composition and distributing projects.

Here are the key activities associated with record taking care of in Python:

Opening a Document:
To communicate with a record, you should initially open it. Python

gives the open() capability for this reason. You can indicate the document's name and mode ('r' for perusing, 'w' for composing, 'a' for adding, and so on.).

```python
Duplicate code
document = open("example.txt", "r")
```

Perusing from a Document:
To peruse the substance of a document, you can utilize techniques like read(), readline(), or readlines().

```python
Duplicate code
content = file.read()
```

Keeping in touch with a Document:
To make or change a document, you can open it in compose mode and

use techniques like compose() to add content.

```python
Duplicate code
record = open("new_file.txt", "w")
file.write("This is some text.")
```

Shutting a Document:

It's fundamental for close a record after you've completed the process of working with it. You can do this utilizing the nearby() strategy.

```python
Duplicate code
file.close()
```

Annexing to a Document:

To add content to a current record without overwriting its ongoing substance, you can open it in add mode ('a').

```python
```

Duplicate code

```
document = open("existing_file.txt", "a")
file.write("This text will be added to the furthest limit of the document.")
```

With Articulation (Setting Supervisor):

Python upholds the utilization of the with proclamation, which consequently shuts the document when you're finished with it. It's a more helpful method for taking care of documents.

python
Duplicate code

```
with open("example.txt", "r") as document:
    content = file.read()
# Document is consequently shut here
```

Blunder Dealing with:

While working with records, urgent to deal with special cases could happen, for example, document not found or authorization issues. You can involve attempt with the exception of blocks for this.

```python
Duplicate code
attempt:
    document = open("non_existent_file.txt", "r")
but FileNotFoundError:
    print("The record doesn't exist.")
```

Working with Text Records:
For text records, it's frequently valuable to peruse or compose line by line. You can utilize a for circle to repeat through the lines.

```python
Duplicate code
```

```python
with open("text_file.txt", "r") as document:
    for line in document:
        print(line)
```

Make sure to apply these document taking care of procedures in your composition and distributing projects on a case by case basis, whether you're working with content, information, or design records. Legitimate document the board is fundamental to keep up with the trustworthiness of your work.

High level Points in python

Decorators: Python decorators permit you to change the way of behaving of capabilities or techniques. They are frequently utilized for undertakings like logging, approval, and memoization. Understanding decorators can assist you with composing more secluded and clean code.

Generators and Iterators: These are fundamental for effective memory the board and working with enormous datasets. Generators make iterators, and they can be an integral asset while managing successions of information.

Metaclasses: Metaclasses give a method for characterizing the design and conduct of classes. They are especially helpful for building structures or authorizing coding guidelines in your tasks.

Simultaneousness and Parallelism: Python furnishes different ways of working with strings and cycles for simultaneous and equal programming. The stringing and multiprocessing modules are fundamental in this unique situation.

Asyncio: Assuming that you're keen on offbeat programming, the asyncio library permits you to compose offbeat, non-hindering code, which can be exceptionally helpful for building responsive applications.

Terminations and Extensions: Understanding how Python handles variable extensions and terminations is pivotal for composing hearty and viable code. It's a principal idea in Python's capability based approach.

Normal Articulations: Customary articulations are an incredible asset for text handling. Knowing how to utilize them really can be a critical resource while managing text-based information.

High level Information Designs: Python gives a few high level information structures like sets, namedtuples, and defaultdicts that can make your code more effective and expressive.

Information bases and ORM: Assuming you're associated with web improvement or information driven applications, understanding how to work with data sets, including utilizing Article Social Planning (ORM) libraries like SQLAlchemy, is critical.

Testing and Investigating: High level testing strategies, for example, unit testing, ridiculing, and test-driven improvement (TDD), can assist with guaranteeing the quality and dependability of your code.

Go ahead and let me know as to whether you might want to investigate any of these subjects in more detail or on the other hand on the off chance that you have a particular inquiry connected with your composition or distributing work.

- Python is a flexible programming language that is broadly utilized in web improvement because of its straightforwardness, comprehensibility, and a broad scope of libraries.
- Web Systems: Python has a few web systems that improve on the advancement interaction. Two of the most famous ones are Django and Cup.

- Django: Django is an undeniable level Python web structure that follows the "batteries-included" reasoning. It gives a ton of implicit usefulness, including an administrator board, client confirmation, and an ORM

(Article Social Planning) framework. This settles on it an extraordinary decision for bigger, more intricate tasks.

- Flask: Flagon is a miniature system, and that implies it's more moderate and gives you more command over the parts you need to utilize. It's incredible for more modest undertakings and models.

- Information base Reconciliation: Python flawlessly coordinates with different information bases. You can involve SQLite for lightweight applications, PostgreSQL, MySQL, or even NoSQL data sets like

MongoDB relying upon your task's necessities.

- Front-end Advancements: To make drawing in sites, you'll have to utilize HTML, CSS, and JavaScript related to Python. Libraries like Jinja2 are generally utilized for templating to insert Python code inside HTML layouts.

- Soothing APIs: Python can be utilized to assemble Serene APIs that permit your web applications to associate with outer administrations or different applications.

- Deployment: There are a few choices for conveying your Python web applications.

Well known decisions incorporate stages like Heroku, AWS, or setting up your own server utilizing Nginx and Gunicorn or uWSGI.

- Content Administration Frameworks (CMS): Assuming you're engaged with distributing, you should seriously think about utilizing Python-based CMS like Wagtail or Mezzanine, which can work on happy administration and distributing.

- Security: Web security is essential. Python has libraries like OWASP's Security Information System (SKF) and different confirmation structures to assist with getting your applications.

- Scalability: Consider how your site will scale as your readership develops. Python is reasonable for both little and huge ventures, however you'll have to pursue design choices considering versatility.

- SEO: Website improvement is fundamental for distributers. Python libraries like Delightful Soup and Scrapy can help you scratch and dissect information for Website design enhancement improvement.

- Content Conveyance: While distributing content, a Substance Conveyance Organization (CDN) can assist with conveying content to clients quicker. Python can be utilized to oversee and mechanize CDN-related assignments.

- Make sure to keep your substance unique and connecting with, as your job as an essayist and distributer isn't just about the specialized parts of web improvement yet additionally making content that dazzles your crowd. Furthermore, obviously, consistently guarantee to follow best

practices and keep away from
literary theft in your work.

Python for Information Science

Python's part in information science can be extensively separated into the accompanying regions:

Information Control: Python offers libraries like NumPy and Pandas that are fundamental for information control. You can talk about how these libraries empower the treatment of enormous datasets, information cleaning, and change.

Information Representation: Matplotlib and Seaborn are amazing assets for making information representations. Make sense of how these libraries can help in making clever diagrams, charts, and plots to convey information drifts really.

AI: Python's Scikit-Learn library is broadly utilized for building AI models. Examine the meaning of this in information science and give instances of true applications.

Profound Learning: TensorFlow and PyTorch are famous for profound learning projects. You can investigate how these libraries are reforming fields like picture acknowledgment, regular language handling, from there, the sky is the limit.

Information Investigation: Talk about the significance of Jupyter note pads for intuitive information investigation and how it works with coordinated effort among information researchers.

Information Source Incorporation: Python can interface with different information sources, including data sets and web APIs. Make sense of how this ability is important in information science projects.

Measurable Investigation: Python's SciPy library is fundamental for cutting edge measurable investigation. You can expand on its part in theory testing, relapse examination, from there, the sky is the limit.

Enormous Information: Python can likewise deal with large information projects utilizing libraries like PySpark. Share bits of knowledge into how Python squeezes into the large information biological system.

Information Morals: Feature the significance of information morals in information science projects, including issues like information security and predisposition. You should cover how Python helps address these worries.

Profession in Information Science with Python: Offer direction on how people can fabricate a vocation in information science utilizing Python, including suggested learning ways and assets.

Make sure to introduce true models, contextual investigations, and commonsense tips that can hold any importance with your perusers as both an essayist and distributer. This approach will make your substance seriously captivating and educational.

Conclusion:

- Documentation: As a matter of some importance, guarantee your code is legitimate. Use remarks to make sense of the motivation behind your capabilities, factors, and any intricate rationale. This helps you as well as any future designers who would chip away at your code.

- Testing: Run intensive tests to guarantee your code capabilities true to form. Check for edge cases and handle potential mistakes nimbly. Troubleshoot any issues that might emerge during testing.

- Code Cleanup: Prior to finishing up your code, ensure it's perfect and coordinated. Eliminate any repetitive or unused code. This further develops comprehensibility as well as assists with upkeep.

- Execution Streamlining: If necessary, upgrade your code for execution. This could include tweaking calculations, lessening memory use, or further developing execution speed.

- Blunder Taking care of: Guarantee that your code handles special cases and blunders smoothly. Use attempt aside from blocks to forestall crashes and give significant mistake messages.

- Following stages:
- Adaptation Control: Consider utilizing a rendition control framework like Git. This permits you to follow changes, team up with others, and effectively return to past forms if fundamental.

- Code Survey: In the event that you're working with a group, direct code surveys. This aides in tracking down expected issues, further developing code quality, and sharing information.

- Documentation for Clients: Assuming your code is

intended to be utilized by others, make easy to understand documentation. Clarify how for utilize your code, what it does, and give models.

- Input and Emphasis: Share your code with others and assemble criticism. Utilize this criticism to constantly repeat and work on your code.

- Scaling and Upkeep: Plan for what's to come. In the event that your code is essential for a bigger undertaking, contemplate how it will scale and what upkeep will be required.

- Security Contemplations: Contingent upon your venture, consider safety efforts to safeguard against weaknesses and information breaks.

- Deployment: On the off chance that your code is expected for creation use, plan its organization. This might include setting up servers, arranging information bases, and guaranteeing versatility.

- Learned: Remain refreshed with the most recent advancements in Python and related innovations. Learning is a consistent cycle in the realm of programming.

- Keep in mind, closing your Python code is only one stage in the excursion of programming advancement. Viable preparation and following stages are fundamental for guaranteeing the achievement and life span of your task. Blissful coding!

Index

In Python, the add() strategy is fundamentally used to add components to records. Records are a flexible information structure that permits you to store assortments of things. This is the way you can utilize add():

The add() technique is explicitly intended for records. It permits you to add components to the furthest limit of a rundown, expanding its length. For example, suppose you have a vacant rundown:

```python
Duplicate code
my_list = []
```

To add components to this rundown, you can utilize annex(). For instance:

python
Duplicate code
```python
my_list.append(1)
my_list.append(2)
my_list.append(3)
```
In the wake of executing these lines, my_list will contain [1, 2, 3]. The add() strategy is particularly valuable when you need to powerfully fabricate a rundown by adding components as your program runs.

Here is a more reasonable model. Suppose you need to gather client information and store it in a rundown:

python
Duplicate code
```python
user_responses = []
while Valid:
```

```python
    reaction = input("Enter something (or 'q' to stop): ")
    if reaction == 'q':
        break
```

```python
user_responses.append(response)
```

In this code, the annex() strategy adds the client's contribution to the user_responses list until they choose to stop by entering 'q'.

This is an essential prologue to utilizing add() in Python, and it's an incredible asset for building and changing records in your projects. In the event that you have a particular inquiries or need more subtleties on a connected point, if it's not too much trouble, go ahead and inquire.

www.ingramcontent.com/pod-product-compliance
Lightning Source LLC
Chambersburg PA
CBHW071101260726

48661CB00006B/2388